Slow Walk Home

SAINT JULIAN PRESS

POETRY

Praise for *Slow Walk Home*

"In Nussey's sequence of poems, remembrance and domesticity expand organically into transcendence, a thoughtful woman's love of family and memory enlarged – in a moment, without labor or academics – to include God and Time and things yet unseen. Small things here are emblems of the great. The temporary is a palpable fragment of Eternity. Think of John Donne's daughter through many generations, fully modern, yet standing upon the same dark diamond."

~David Brendan Hopes
Peniel and *The Ones with Difficult Names*

"In *Slow Walk Home*, the sacred and the ordinary meet to create a world that is both exquisitely intimate and quietly transcendent. Gradually, the poet reveals a life that is burdened by secrets and animated by mystery. Her poems, with their matter-of-fact tone and their unique and surprising metaphors, never flinch from the experiences they explore: death, illness, loss, doubt...motherhood, love, faith, redemption. Graciously, Nussey opens a door, guiding us into and through an inner sanctum lit by luminous language and lucid vision."

~Laura Budofsky Wisniewski
Sanctuary, Vermont
Orison Poetry Prize winner

"Without minimizing the complexity of the past, *Slow Walk Home* examines the narrow promises of mid-century social expectations against the speaker's and the reader's present-day awareness. The complacency of middle-class back yards is shattered by an air-raid siren; a stay-at-home mom protects her son by means of a heroic lie; mother-daughter bonds are tested and reforged; and a longing for spiritual certitude is relentlessly interrogated by doubt. Readers who recall the Cold War and feminism's Second Wave will find much to recognize in this collection, which offers a deeply personal and illuminating window into the influences of the recent past."

~Anne Marie Todkill
Orion Sweeping

"*Slow Walk Home* is a work of spiritual autobiography that accords its subject grace: that is to say, it turns away neither from her dignity nor from her abjection. It is brave. It is also, in moments, prayerful, using the technology of verse to wring the meanings from a set of simple phrases. We can meditate in and with it. Suzanne Nussey is undeniably a religious poet, as devout as she is heterodox – in tune with a tradition she is also radically remaking."

~Luke Hathaway
The Affirmations and *Years, Months, Days*

Slow Walk Home

Poems

by

Suzanne Nussey

SAINT JULIAN PRESS
HOUSTON

Published by
SAINT JULIAN PRESS, Inc.
2053 Cortlandt, Suite 200
Houston, Texas 77008

www.saintjulianpress.com

Paperback ISBN-13: 978-1-955194-29-7
eBook EPUB ISBN: 978-1-955194-30-3
Library of Congress Control Number: 2024939384

Cover Art Credit: *Moonlit Serenity* by Evelina Parabina

For my family, then and now

CONTENTS

SAFE AS HOUSES

Body my house
my horse my hound
what will I do
when you are fallen

~May Swenson, "Question"

Slow Walk Home

MY FATHER'S HOUSE

What came of picking flowers

Early in the morning, I find the gladiolas
in silver pails of water stored
on the cool floor of my father's garden shed.
Their flowers, miniature angels
the size of my small hand,
climb bright green swords
until the crowning buds furl
into creamy fists.

How my father loves his garden
behind the church and manse
on the border of the woods
where I am not allowed to go.
Now its scant August bed
awaits September blooms.
I free the perfect flowers
from their metal pails, planting them
in ranks of rebel angels, until
his garden blossoms brilliantly again
and I see my work is good.

When the sun is high,
my father calls from the shed.
Who has seen his flowers for the wedding
in the afternoon? My mother answers:
costly hothouse glads, the lateness
of the hour, an angry bride.
And then she calls my name.
Hands stained brown and green
with blame, I run to the woods,
wordless to explain

love's imperfect work,
flowers without gardens,
the reason for this ruin.

My father finds the gladiolas,
swords listing, wings soiled, fists unfurled,
swooning like a tipsy heavenly host that cannot fly.
From my hiding place, I watch
his hands that tend the garden,
his lips that will not lie.
He steps back and shades his eyes.
He sees me. And then
he laughs.

The magic fan

1
The congregation beats time
double to the rhythm
of the preacher's tired voice.
With cheap grass fans
they chase the August heat
back and forth in unison
lifting limp wisps
of sweat-damped hair.
Mothers hush restless children
suctioning sticky thighs
against the varnished pews.
A bat dives through
the open window
sinks in the drowsy air
spins out again
to the street empty
in heat-stricken twilight.

2
Past sundown the manse next door
never cools. Upstairs
we sleep in our underwear
on starched sheets.
My mother in a frayed robe,
modest even in the heat,
holds a sequined fan,
black lace stitched to ebony.
Sent from France, she says,
from her brother in the war.

Nothing in this house
is like the black fan.

She spreads its carved ribs
like the wing of a wild bird.
She sweeps the air
and in a voice she never brings

next door she sings
how the black fan
will vanish summer
and winter and spring
and then the worn out year.
Her frail wrist freed
from the robe's long sleeve
works the raven fan like a conjuror

before her final verse
sends us wandering
into the fantastic night.

3
High in a loft bed, airtight
in our air-conditioned bungalow,
my daughter sleeps
beyond the season's reach
beyond street noise and heat,
needing nothing
a mother might supply.

I close our bedroom door and raise
in secret the double hung window
above the bed as high as it will go.
I wait for the old forgotten fever
to find me and the black fan
I have summoned from its resting place
in my perfumed drawer.

The wicked fairy at the cradle

An old-time preacher takes
my father's Sunday evening service
when my mother's water breaks
and they bolt for the hospital
before anyone can wish them
well or offer prayers or cast a spell
for me. But all hell breaks loose
when the old man shames the organist
for her jewelry forbidden
in his books, and she counters
with invective from King James:
Viper, fool, blind guide,
hypocrite, whitewashed grave full
of dead men's bones,
extortionist of human souls.
The congregation then takes sides,
making it a full-on fight
ending only when the man in charge
of music puts his trumpet
to his lips, blasting "Silent Night"
so loud my grandmother next door
can sing along.
Thus my advent is heralded
with a curse, a battle, and a song.

Cant

play cards swim bike
wear shorts on Sunday
smoke dance drink or
go to movies. Ever.
I complain. How to understand
this law forbidding lipstick
pierced ears tight pants
sleeveless dresses Schlitz
Pale Ale Virginia Slims
commercials on TV?
It's the devil says my mother
in the details
even I can't explain.

In my father's house

a thin glass jar sits on a shelf
in a deep closet behind the organ
to the left of a tall window
and the big wooden chairs
with high carved backs where
my father sits before he stands to pray
or preach behind the great oak stand
that holds his books and papers.

Worn red hymnals
and soft black Bibles stamped
with gold sit in the deep closet
in my father's house.
On the shelves beside them
rest round brass plates lined
with green felt to keep coins quiet;
woven grass fans shaped
like hearts with handles;
silver trays hollowed
to hold glass thimbles
of Jesus' blood;
and flat silver platters for the small
hard slivers of the body of our Lord
kept in cardboard boxes
in the deep closet facing
rows of empty benches
in the house where I play alone.

In the thin glass jar
in the deep closet, ghost fish
the size of minnows float
in resin that makes their rose-gold
scales shimmer when I hold them to the light.

Their eyes are silver sequins filled
with black beads staring through the walls
of the thin glass jar on the shelf.
Many times I ask my father
why he keeps dead things in the closet
with the songs and books and plates
and supper for the Lord.
His answer stays the same.

He does not know what they are.
They do not belong to him.
I should not play with them.
So they must stay in this house

where I am afraid to venture
past the thin glass jar
to the back of the dark closet
that holds a mystery
my father cannot name.

The old camera, 1956

The camera sees a bed, a nightstand, a window. The nightstand holds a small glass fish bowl and a low round tank for turtles. Dark sailboats drift across the curtained window only partly in the camera's view. Two boys, nine and one, and a small girl, three, sit upright in bed against the centre panel of the metal headboard embossed with pale hearts and curlicues. The nine-year-old wears cowboy pajamas. His arm circles the little boy, who holds a toy stuffed dog. The small girl leans away from the boys to the edge of the viewfinder's frame, as though she might be leaving. The youngest child stares into the camera, surprised; the girl is laughing; the oldest boy smiles widely. His short hair shines, as if it has just been washed. The toddler's fine fuzz stands straight up like dandelion down. The girl's hair is rolled in tiny curlers, wrapped in a bandana circling the crown of her head. It might be Saturday night or Sunday morning, the children prepped for church.

There is much the children do not see. The older boy doesn't see the three-year-old take his pet turtles out of their bowl to hold and stroke them. One day she will crush them in her eager little grasp. He hasn't seen his guppies eat their young shortly after birth. When the fry vanish, he will blame the other children. The toddler does not see the little girl, lured by his stuffed dog's soft fur and shiny glass eyes, as she practices stealing it from his crib when he falls asleep, then carefully putting it back.

None of them sees the man who stands below their window at night to ask for money. They do not see their father rising early every day to give himself a shot of insulin before breakfast. Or if the shot is not enough, their mother crying when he slurs his words and staggers. Though the nine-year-old has practiced drills for air-raids, none of the children have seen photos of Hiroshima's ruins. They cannot see what conspires to make their world, children and grownups, weekdays and Sundays, good guys and bad, us and them, heaven and hell, now and eternity.

They have not seen what will keep them together or what will take them apart.

The youngest son

Never a father yourself,
you harp on the harms
our parents did us: too much
Lawrence Welk and Jesus,
not enough Dylan and D. H.;
Noxema on sunburn,
pasta from cans.
Now they are shadows
answering only
to what we wanted them to be.

Shall they wring their hands
for all eternity,
blame themselves
for the day you tore
the freezer door from its hinges
when it lacked what you wanted
for the meal that you had planned?

Lucky charms

We did not play well together.
Except on nights we couldn't sleep,
our parents downstairs still
cleaning up the day. Awake
in bed, we made a game
of conjuring feasts from the lexicon
of our few years. Condensed
milk, Cream of Wheat, brown sugar;
roast beef, potatoes baked. Gravy.
We incanted sweets, apple pie,
rainbow Jell-O, chocolate parfait.
We charmed each other,
fell asleep, imaginations full,
no fights, no tears.

I hunger
in these daylight hours
for that nighttime spell
we worked against all hurt.

The oldest son leaves home

Cold war

We're playing fort in the garage attic
when the air-raid siren
begins its ascent to full-pitched keen.
You tell me to hide
under Dad's Chevrolet Two-ten.
You say duck and cover
like we do in school.
Wait, you tell me, *till it's safe to come out*.
I believe that day you love me.

So I lie face down on the cement floor,
arms crossed over my head.
I taste oil and dust.
When I call, you do not answer.
I cannot see you leave.
I wonder if this is the end
of the world our father preaches.

I keep my place until long after the siren
has ceased its fearful wailing
and our mother calls my name.

I never hear from you.
I believe you have forgotten me.

Moving day

Our father stands at the threshold
of the emptied manse.
Placing both hands
on the freshly washed walls,
he walks from room to vacant room,
palming the inward perimeter
like a potter steadily
unmaking his art
with each turn of the wheel.

In the laneway,
the Dodge Dart idles.
You wait, impatient,
at the wheel.

Red, white, blue

It's a small town and the bus
to Buffalo stops just once a week.
You are watching for it now,
out front of the White Hawk Inn
on US Route 19.
Anyone could see you
sitting there alone on the red bench,
the only passenger from home,
waiting for a ride
to your life without us.

Four blocks away,
our mother who never lies,
not even the smallest white ones,
stands at our front door, arms crossed,
confronting the stranger with Brylcreemed hair,
a badge and blue business suit,
who wonders where you are.
She plays simple folk
and keeps him talking, the agent
fumbling to bring it to an end.

Soon you will pick up Dad's old suitcase
and board that beat-up Bluebird
to Canada, travelling north
until your trail goes cold.

For years, I cannot say where you have gone.

Borders

Your daughter hands her newborn
over the altar's threshold
into your holy space.
The infant rests easily
in the white linen crèche
of your slight arms.
You dip your practised hand
into the stone font, lave
and towel the tiny skull, righting
her tipped soul with a quick swipe
of holy oil across her brow.
You smile into the baby's startled face.

How you conjure our father
who drove his Buick Skylark north
to baptize your own son and daughters
after you refused to take up arms
in an unholy war.

Your gray eyes, dim behind glasses,
resurrect his
watching from afar
as though he were stepping back,
stepping back to see us clearly
before his last long trip
across the border.

Selfie with Jesus: The Light of the World

(After Holman Hunt)

Have you always been backdrop,
just off to the left,
slightly out of focus?
Behind me,
where I sat as a child
at the kitchen table,
you held a lantern
knocked at a door?
a window? a mirror?
covered with vines.
My mother said
it was my heart.
Even now
you look lonely.

The story of the girl who went forth
to learn fear
(After the Brothers Grimm)

-1-

From far away, the woman's family travels in winter to the house where her mother lies ill. When they arrive, a nurse bars them from the old woman's bedside, worried their presence might frighten her patient. The distraught daughter waits outside the room, holding her baby girl in an old rocking chair, a family heirloom. She will rock and weep until her mother dies.

But the story begins earlier: The old woman sits by the newborn's crib while her daughter rests on the sofa downstairs. She fights off her own drowsiness to check on the sleeping child. The left side of the infant's small body has gone strangely blue. Even when the old woman turns her, the baby does not stir. The old woman shouts for her daughter as she lifts the baby from its deep womb of slumber. She rocks her in long, swooping arcs, over and over calling the child's name.

Until the baby cries and is born again.

-2-

On a wooded path where, for years, she has walked safely from the valley to her house, the young girl meets a snake. Rattlers and water moccasins are common here, but they stay closer to the river. This is an Eastern racer, long, muscular, and famously swift. Its dark body rises like an old rope come to life from under wet leaves layered across the forest floor. She runs; the snake pursues. When they reach the dusty road at the top of the hill, the racer halts and slides back into the damp shadows that keep it secret.

She wonders whether it is her terror or the snake's that is crisp on her tongue.

-3-

Still married, she sleeps alone in a single bed in the spare room. Tonight her husband's voice like a troubling dream flushes her out of sleep's safe cover. She finds him in the kitchen, staring at the spackled ceiling, scolding a partner she cannot see. She cannot touch him. She makes hot chocolate, scalds milk in a battered aluminum pot. Making small talk, she asks about his parents' boat, the book he's reading. She asks, What's new? He answers in clipped sentences. She turns to find him standing at the cutlery drawer. He lifts the Cutco knife her cousin sent for their wedding. A quality knife, reliably sharpened, *the most useful gift you'll ever get*, her cousin wrote. Her husband stares at the knife as though he does not know it, turns it over twice, and dully remarks, *Sometimes I hate you.*

-4-

She pulls into the conservation area around three, enough time for a short hike before the January light completely abandons this dull afternoon. A mud-spattered, black Ford pick-up, back bumper wired on, rusted front fender the colour of dried blood, is the only presence in the lot. In the truck's cargo bed, a dented washing machine leans against the tailgate like a toppled white headstone. A skiff of snow covers the ground. One set of footprints leads into the forest. In other cities and towns, three million women are marching. She throws her backpack in the trunk, locks the car doors, and pockets her keys. The light in the gray sky holds. She walks toward the woods.

Slow walk home

In the beginning,
there is a rain-washed street,
the spice of bridal wreath
spirea. From the parsonage
we walk to bigger houses,
bright without, dark within,
parishioners my father visits weekly.

On dust-pocked, thickly painted
porches, they greet us.
Their silver hair coiled
into mesh-capped knots.
Their brown shoes sturdy. Like me
they smell of soap and talcum.
I see something in their faces
I do not recognize.
My father talks
in his quiet voice.
They fill my hands with hard
candy when we leave.

On our slow walk home
my father keeps me
upright in my soft leather shoes
over pebbled sidewalk slabs, heaved
and tilted like a drawbridge rising.
He promises the black dog
barking will not bite.
He names for me
the things I do not know.
Shepherd. Sparrow. Oak.
Blossom. Widow.

Everything new. This day
an empty tablet not yet tipped
toward calamity.
Just now
  the face of my father
  turned toward me
   the blissful season
   opening its arms
       Come this way, this way, this

LIFE SKILLS

Selfie with Jesus: Church

In an Anglican church on Bay,
a white-haired priest intones
the psalm that breaks my heart.
My father's God
has not kept his word.
Sad, alone, and out of work
in this strange town, I am shocked
to see you there beside me
squarely in the frame, saying,
The next part is hard, I fear.
Or is it, *The old fart's*
hard to hear?
I understand
it's not a joke.

Toward my mother

What she told me:
whistling girls, crowing hens always come to no good end marry rich if
you don't want to clean never let anyone thin your hair don't swallow
melon seeds they'll root in your stomach and grow always leave home
in respectable underwear in case you are taken to hospital suddenly
what you're looking for will be gone if you wait for sales you can catch
a bird by salting its tail
which I tried.

She must be laughing
still.
I wait for sales.
Though married twice, I clean
my own house, sometimes
with help.
I spit out seeds.
I whistle bird songs,
first practised
at nap time in school,
sending me home
early.
I own ten pair
of cotton underwear,
have been to hospital
three times,
once suddenly.
But who dared to thin
my young mother's thick
hair that stayed rich
auburn until sickness turned

its curls cast-iron, salted
them with white, and finally hid
their absence
under a clean cotton cap?

What she never said:
I am lost.

Her only friends
her sisters
five-hundred miles away.

Her work
the three of us
oblivious.

Her husband
devoted devout distracted
weekdays and Sunday.

Her talents
under-estimated unsung
unrecompensed.

Her fear
dismissed
disabling.

I did not know
how to listen
and cannot find her now.

Life skills (1): Clean breaks

I had a gift for pithing.
My lab mates brought me
frogs they couldn't bear to kill.
I dispatched them quickly:
nerve muscle bone
clean precise forever.
At fifteen
my grasp of suffering
was so small.

Where is the perfect spot
to sink the probe,
snap the cord
linking
me to you,
painlessly sever every
longing impulse thought
so firmly holding
me in thrall?
My aptitude for leaving
is so small.

Metamorphosis

In nova fert animus
mutatas dicere formas corpora

I thought I saw
everything
but you turned
when I was not looking
    your face fixed
        like a wax museum doll
    your eyes naked as a fish
    unfathomable dull

Now I cannot find
    you to say
farewell so
I sing
    of the shape shifting
    creatures you once loved
We all turn
    into something else

Watch me
    slip my skin
    and swim away

Travel in the after times

I wake before birdsong,
my thoughts in vertical dive.
You've been gone for years.

Dangerous to travel now
by air. Too far by land.
How can we meet
when we cannot
cross the border?

Migratory songbirds
are dropping from the skies
by thousands.
No one knows why.

Selfie with Jesus: I and Thou

It's Beer and Pizza Sunday
when you walk in with Chet,
my friend the priest.
We order a thin-crust
meat-lover's like we used to
with my ex. I tell him
how the marriage ended after nothing
worked—therapy, yoga, church.
 "I'm sorry," I confess,
keeps going through my head.
You interrupt, as you often do.
That, you say, *is me.*
It's not always about you.
So I order you a beer, and Chet
picks up the check.

On your way out, please close the door behind you

Everything works its way
to naught
relentlessly as surf on stone
    bones soften
    retinas tear
    cells rebel proliferate decay
       surgeries sever
       tissue from tumour
           fever wastes what's healthy
           and what's not.
              The body erodes.
                We melt away.

So too our flesh and blood
depart, make a plan
    to split   the instant
    they're conceived.
       The rift grows subtly
       until this drift
           pulls a continent apart

           and all connection
           cleaves until

              the body

               becomes nothing

               but another

               body's
                 thought.

Deliquescence

Beginning the removal of her
substance from the earth
sweat pearls her brow
imitates her baptism
soaks her cotton gown.
Already she is less
than my mother
dissolving from the small bones
that buoyed her through eight ill seasons.

Not now.

Her final words reproach
my wish to change her
gown for something soft and dry.
I have misjudged the element she navigates
while the nurse and I
attempt to dress her
as though she were an infant or a doll.
How are we to fathom
what she requires now?

Morphine
melts her into senselessness
beyond dreaming. Breath sinks
deeper in her body ebbing
even as she becomes a flood
drowning sheets hair skin
the flannel we have swaddled her in.

Water poured her into life.
Water carries her away.

Nocturne

Outside the hospital window, July fireworks bloom over treetops on the night horizon. For hours I have stayed by my mother's bed. Sometimes we talk; often she dozes. Earlier we listened to the *Four Last Songs* on the radio. I wonder if she knew them. My mother is dying. This evening she said her last goodbyes to my husband and daughter. Now she asks to sleep.

How clearly she desires her end. How long she has worked to accomplish it as she has wanted: following doctors' orders, not burdening her children, not complaining, refusing drugs that cloud her mind and fool her body. She has earned the rest she longs for.

A volley of fireworks, barely audible on our side of the hospital wall, explodes with the soft pop of an impatiens dispersing its seed. I watch my mother, who has fallen asleep.

I must not lose my way in this silence.

A voice, weedy and diminished, startles me. My mother is singing Brahms' *Lullaby*. Her voice comes from far away, a spooky imitation of the voice that sang at my bedside when I was a child, or more somberly in church. This small voice twists like smoke toward the ceiling of her room
and vanishes.

Haiku for my mother

On the day she dies
though she is a well sunk deep
no tears wet her eyes.

Seasonal disorder

September pulls in like a mother late
to pick up children after school.
Quick, no time to waste, just
five minutes to cross town
for soccer, groceries,
supper, dance for the rest
of someone else's life.

Once again, it leaves
without her. Too sad, too sick,
too slow. What will it be this time?
Every year she says, *This time*
I will look for work,
write my book, exercise,
meditate, stop
worrying,
get   some   help.

She sees her sad, untidy house.
Its dusty windows dim
her unattended garden;
Important documents
she will not consult again
have overgrown her desk.
She thinks of her industrious friends –
poets, teachers, priests –
how hard she has worked
at nothing and nothing
worked.
Then she does not run, write,
apply, be patient,
pray.

In the abandoned schoolyard,
a truant wind spins dust
over the empty swings that sway
as though some daring child has just leapt out
into the uncomplicated air,
travelling away
from the trampled grass below.

The passion of St. Agatha

They take your shoes,
your clothes, your ring
and leave you
with a thin, ill-fitting gown
and your name written
incorrectly on a paper bracelet.
A woman lets you keep
the shawl your mother knitted.
You slip a tiny portrait
of your daughter into the band
around your wrist.
Then you wait
in a room, windowless
as a cell.

When you are cool to the touch,
they wheel you down a dim corridor
to an unlit chamber.
Two women in men's clothing
remove your shawl and scroll
your gown to your waist.
They lead you to a metal platform
where you must stand and clutch
the machine that sees your death.
They pull and twist your naked breast
between two silver plates
until a clamp locks
the kneaded flesh in place.
You wait.

A man enters the room
and will not look at your face.
The women hand him

long metal wires
which he examines.
The man adjusts the screen
attached to the silent machine.
He tells you not to breathe.
Slowly he threads one wire
into your breast.
This he repeats three times.
Your breast on the screen
is alive with steel teeth
that will tell another man
where to dock his knife.

The man leaves the room.
The women tape paper
crowns like bakers' toques
over the wires on your breast.
They dress you in the thin gown.
Your shawl has disappeared.
The baby remains hidden
in your left wrist.
They leave. You wait
alone in the dark place.

You are led
to the final room
where two men in white caps
spread your body on a table.
Four attending women strap
your arms perpendicular to your body,
palms up
on cool steel plates.

One man buries a tube in the hand
where your baby hides;
the other drops
a mask over your face,
commanding you to breathe deeply.
When your eyes no longer open,

you dream you walk barefoot
in red velvet robes,
bearing your orphaned breasts
like scored loaves of warm bread
on a plain wooden platter
to feed the children of the countless poor.

Life skills (2): Extravagance

For Charles

He came from up the valley.
He lived in a shelter downtown.
She taught him life skills and yoga
at the Booth Street Sally Ann.

He made her a brooch of seashells
before he disappeared, a delicate
flower with petals like tear-drops,
the work of a master's hand.

She was paid for what she gave him.
He gave her what was dear.

Revenant

You come and go from us
like my dead mother in dreams:
parent, child,
the furniture of memory
not yet erased.
Meals together, goodnights exchanged,
never doubting that good mornings
take their place.

Last week a storm took down
the old maple by our house,
steadfast eighty years, toppled
in one night. Just days before your birth,
in the shadow of its canopy
(bare the day you were conceived)
I lay against its base
to hold the weight of you
I could scarcely bear standing.
How like death birth is, I supposed,
something the body knows
to do without
the mind's instruction,
pushing past thought
to whatever end its DNA received.
No revising the code
that drives you from us now.
Like my mother's, your visitations
are diminished, then withdrawn.

What anguish when I wake
and find the loved one
gone.

Selfie with Jesus: Another country

Wedding photos show your portrait
hanging in the archway where we wait
to walk her down the aisle.
You elevate an oblong Host high
before your eyes, and smile.
The pianist segues from Elvis
to Bach, the congregation stands,
and we begin our family trip
taking love to the altar
in this unfamiliar land.
Where you pose for your sacramental
selfie in its canvas air,
can you hear my parting prayer?
Lord.
Have mercy.

The mother of the bride remembers
her first marriage

You ask me for a poem
for your wedding day.
I say,
I cannot do it.
I cannot gloss
so grand a theme.

There is another truth.
I recall a lonely girl
considering
her dive into waters
veiled by shadow playing
off their troubled skin.
Stay on shore! Don't do it!
the only words that scan.
I can, she says,
and plunges in.

Lacuna

The first time I knew
that you were here
I felt a subtle ripple
vis vitae
then hiccups rolling
waves of you a fist
thrust to my heart
a pressure on my back
fellow traveler
navigating inner space.

When you first knew me
as more than mother ship
muffled sound and distant
songs in your amniotic sea
was I someone like yourself
or a creature from your fetal dreams
materializing
before your newborn eyes
as though you
had just birthed me?

Though I no longer
can contain you
nothing else so well
contents these arms
that lifted you that day
to see my face.
There are no words
to take that space.

Life skills (3): Maximal density packing

During their sixties her husband learns to make a golden
loaf open crumb – tall rise straight sides smooth top. Then
pies. Then cake. She gives up baking throws in the towel at
dinnertime. Abandons all domestic chores keeping just the
garden and the wash. And packing. Dishwasher freezer
trunk her suitcase. Here she excels which she attributes to
an aptitude for rearranging space discovered during grade
five math. *How many unit cubes fit a solid square?* Will spend
her later life writing verse and placing everything she lost
into small spaces.

SAFE AS HOUSES

The music of the house

Compared to the larger harm
our first parents did,
the family home swapped
for a mouthful of fruit,
Augustine's spin on original sin
was no more than a silly riff.
When Uriel placed a fiery sword
at Eden's gate, we all went packing.
You left for school, married,
took a job down south.
I navigate foreign places,
learning complicated tenses,
unfamiliar tunes. Our correspondence
always dwells on home,
a place just glimpsed
when passing by at night
as silhouetted figures move
against a golden light hymning
of a house we cannot find
and cannot forget. A house
in winter almost invisible
but for lamps lit at a door,
reminding us how long ago
we lost our way;
a clapboard house in summer,
where from the darkening road
we hear children laughing
in their beds, whispering
out over the green hedges
away to the dunes and grasses
where the sea listens jealously.
Even in the cabin wilderness
a wild thing pauses

at the murmur of a windowed light.
In such places, waywardly
we've roamed and hoped
this music of the house
might sing us back to home.

Your little house

i.m. Doug, a good neighbour (1946–2015)

The little houses on our street
fall one by one
to fashion or decay,
whatever moves the world along.
The week you left,
another house came down.

We told the stories
that its walls contained
as we watched the backhoe slam
through brick and pane,
peeling memory back,
parlour, kitchen, bath,
until it finally unveiled
the most intimate of spaces.
A life-sized dollhouse
into whose rooms
we placed each vanished
woman, child, and man.
With one wild swing,
the wrecker's arm rammed
the roof and last supporting wall.
The small house caved
like a pricked balloon,
its noisy ruin a hail of grit
that sent us running
and took it back to earth.

You knew the frailty
of mortar, brick and wood,
yet understood what's market value,
what's true worth. Whatever

love and skill can do,
you said, our little houses
will not last. Foundations crumble,
shingles crack; seals blow
and let the cold wind pass.

Even so, you
fixed what you could
until all fixing failed.

Lullaby for an empty nester

You have a bed that loves your bones.
The dog snores softly at your feet,
partnering your partner's drone.
Hermit thrush and tree frog sing
the creeping dark to sleep.
Make a cradle of the night,
a cradle for what's gone.
Nothing to fear
in your twilight.
You are here.
You are home.

Anniversary sonnet

The devouring work of age begun, the long-
awaited daughter of our forties gone
four thousand miles away;
friends' and neighbours' places filled
by strangers who build
gated homes of glass and stone.
One morning they will read
about the lives we led
and observe with faintest praise:
Who would have known?

Milk and sugar at the bottom
of the breakfast bowl,
our meal's substance almost done.
The richest work of love is yet to come.

The dog's ritual

to sit between us on our bed
before we sleep.
Her pink tongue laving
every limb accessible and bare
hands, forehead, neck,
and then, with little moans,
repeat; her devotion
like the Magdalen
anointing Jesus' feet,
speechless to declare
her dread.

Stay.

When you wake at night in terror:
The neurologist's advice
(for Kunda)

Turn the light on.
Read.
If the snakes on the bed remain,
ask a friend to tell you
what they see.

What do you do
when you have no friend nearby
and the snakes won't go away?
What then?

Learn their names.

Lake night

Suspended between our childhood
and whatever old age threatens,
we float on the wooden dock
in an August night, the black
lake lapping beneath us, pinprick
satellites like water bugs
skimming the darkened sky above.

We married men of the same name;
they bracket us on either side.
Yours fusses his portable scope
into focus, seeking meteors.
Mine dozes on a deck chair,
his breath keeping time
with the waves that break below.

Watching them, we rest
in the harbour of the soft night air,
legs tucked like schoolgirls,
star-gazing thoughts adrift
wondering
who will get the pullout couch
and who will get the loft.

On this night, before
the children we will love
more than husbands
break our hearts
as a lover never could, before
losses nest like the wooden dolls
you collect but don't display,
the years you ceased to write or call
and I misunderstood,

when silence is not yet
a troubled place to stop,
I should turn to you and say

if we lose the words for
what happened, what we fear,
how we are strange
to each other and ourselves;
when we are bereft
of instruments to read the present
or divine what is beyond,

I will conjure you
this lake night memory
of the men who love us
more than children,
of silence pure as song,
and pledge never to forsake you
in the night to come.

At seventy

don specs that frame your eyes
as though they were a portrait
by Kahlo or by Klimt.
Purchase many pairs.
Switch them when you've snagged
a stare or conversation.
Go platinum one day;
the next streak your hair
with lavender and black;
style it elegant and swish.
Then shave the back
and ink your skull
with quotes from Kant and Cohen.
Choose tattoos
that state your permanence.

Wear sensible shoes
and Jimmy Choos,
your bra and Depends
over lululemons.
Liberate your haram
breasts; bare
your sun-starved legs.
Flaunt gauzy skirts
that tell secrets
to the wind.
Make yourself a cartoon
character chameleon
some actor's older twin.

Just keep them guessing.

Toward the end
when you tire
of outwardly expressing
your inner crone, do more
than play with numbers.

Reveal everything.
Write to your cousin, friends
who think they know you,
the local paper; tell don't show
the world that never writes to you
what actually happened.

To my right breast before surgery

The left your twin scimitarred
years past the scar hidden
beneath its diminished crescent
you tomorrow flayed and sliced
east to west nipple to breast
bone for the rest of life
the surgeon promises
the ditch cut deep
sweet skin stitched to sweet
incisions fade she says to ghost
skin invisible to all.

Heart sheath
my metaphor
in flesh that lately pleased
my infant and my spouse
and will again be altered
as my hidden self
whose only cure more loss
I am now used to
being carved away.

Let me then be poetry
in bones that keep
my form fifty years
or more entombed
one thousand
in a desert place these bones
whole never wounded
never broken still strong
that lovers' eyes will never
see my enduring self

walk me
home from surgery
hold me upright say
I'm not finished now.

Give me what you have made me

want. Good
work, rest at night
and waking without dread.
Heart to own
this body as my home.
Health for the mind you gave me.
Hope for what you make me
want – a death like nothing
I've imagined darkly
or been taught.

Safe as houses: A litany

The little black ants
of April have arrived.
The bricks
need repointing.
Silver silhouettes
on windows won't deter
incoming birds.
The neighbours are renovating
three feet from our bedroom wall.
Allergies are worse than ever.
Everyone we know
is tired. Four friends
suffer five different cancers:
ovarian, prostate, breast,
bladder, lung. The cross and flag
stand for the gun.

Children in Ukraine
help old women weave
camouflage nets
to mimic green leaves
in spring, yellow
in fall, dirty snow
in winter, praying
May this be the last
time we need them.
Science says
the cruellest season
has already begun.

Help us.

Scavenger angels
Mariupol, The City of Mary, March 2022

Scavenger angels
wheel on heavy wings
over Mariupol, sift
through litter and debris, reject
everything that glitters, glean
only shattered toys, scorched
books, mangled shoes, shredded
bedclothes, slivered
bones gilt in dust,
the last moments
before someone looked up
and knew deliverance
would not come.

Not all angels pass over, arrive
at dinner unannounced, sing
like stars in winter, stand
guard in the garden
of dead Christs.

Scavenger angels
wheel on heavy wings
over Mariupol, silently
lift their treasure from the ashes
like mothers cradling
their injured young
whose suffering's
more radiant than stars,
more sacred than angel song.
They leave no guards
against the misery to come.

First Sunday of Advent

I have stripped my garden
of dead stalks and leaves,
mounded earth over the root balls
of roses and wound them
in rough brown cloth
like a poor woman's child
or a body for the tomb.

Leaf, bird, and light
have flown. The world's
reduced to monochrome,
unornamented lines,
the silent, empty air.
November's difficult truth
is finally laid bare.

I have learned to fear
what looks like death,
to cover all the possibilities
of its approach. (Small catastrophes
have been my coach.) Bad news,
disease and natural disasters
catechize my bleak imagination.

So when the signs say
hunker down,
expect the worst,
I am well-prepared
for mourning,
not for birth.

Winter comes.

Ash Wednesday

I watch you shift your shoulders
troubling your fingers through
your thinning hair the young
girl among us joins our queue
shuffling   silently   forward
in the darkness to receive last Easter's cindered palms a stain
of oil and ashes the ancient verse   *You are dust and to dust you shall return*
The line advances   A crooked cross of ashes
on her brow the child strides from the altar
like a bridesmaid down the aisle dissolving
in the dusty shadows   of God's old house
You take my hand   We leave the way we came

Selfie with Jesus: End times

My godly aunts
were of different minds
about you in the end.
The first time she died,
Mary said, you took
her hand to dance
but the ER doc
convinced her to turn back.
Demons harrowed Doris
on her deathbed
and nothing that you said
could make her less distraught.

I will need a sign.
Something just
the two of us might know.

What I said to my father
the day he taught me how to walk
alone.

Last request

In the end, he said,
we are all alone

when I dreaded leaving home. Strange counsel
from my father who believed in heaven. Yet

at his unexpected end, we all were there:
his wife reciting psalms, his son the priest

in prayer, his youngest prodigal, me
dumbstruck like him, silenced by the pump

that filled his lungs with air.
He penciled in unsteady script

on a paper slip
his hardest words of all.

Don't be afraid.

ACKNOWLEDGMENTS

Earlier versions of these poems have appeared in *EVENT*, *The Mainstreeter*, *The New Quarterly*, *The New Quarterly Blog*, *The Path to Kindness*, *Prairie Fire*, *Stone Canoe*, and *The Windhover*. Many thanks to their editors and staff for the time, care, and space they have given to my work, and to the adjudicators and sponsors of the *EVENT* Non Fiction Contest, The McNally Robinson Booksellers Award, The Nick Blatchford Occasional Verse Contest, and to James Crews, collection editor of *The Path to Kindness*.

THANKS

Slow Walk Home has enjoyed good company along the road to publication. I am deeply grateful to Ron Starbuck for giving my book a welcoming home at Saint Julian Press. Tayve Neese, Caroline Shea, and Anne Marie Todkill guided my book with their insightful and generous editorial skills. And to my comrades in the work of writing – Evelyn Bence, Thomas Gardner, Luke Hathaway, David Hopes, Laura Budofsky Wisniewski, and Linda Mills Woolsey – I owe unending thanks for your support. I especially want to thank poet Anne Marie Todkill, who was the first to say, "This is a book!" For many years now, the Merritt Writers have thoughtfully listened to and helped to shape my work in progress. To my husband and daughter who encourage me to persevere when I am ready to evict the muse and pull up literary stakes: Ken and Sophia, I am always blessed to come home to you.

NOTES

p. 30 "Of bodies changed to various forms, I sing." John Dryden's translation of Ovid, *Metamorphoses* 1:1.

p. 35 "We must not lose our way in this solitude," from "At Gloaming," Joseph von Eichendorff, in Strauss' *Four Last Songs*.

p. 39 St. Agatha was a third-century Christian martyr who suffered many tortures, including having her breasts cut off. She is the patron saint of torture victims, bakers, wet nurses, and breast cancer patients.

p. 64 "Lord, give me what you have made me want," St. Anselm of Canterbury.

p. 66 The title and italicized words are from Stanley Kunitz, "The Layers."

ABOUT THE AUTHOR

Suzanne Nussey holds a M.A. in creative writing from Syracuse University, where she studied under W. D. Snodgrass and Philip Booth. Canadian poet Dennis Lee mentored her at the University of Toronto. She has taught English and writing, earned a M.A. in pastoral counseling, and worked with new Canadians in economic development programs. Her poetry, creative non-fiction, and essays have appeared in a variety of Canadian and US magazines, anthologies, and on-line blogs. Working as a freelance writer and editor in the areas of religion, psychology, and health and wellness, she has also facilitated writing workshops for community groups and for unhoused women. Suzanne lives in Ottawa, Ontario, on the unceded traditional territory of the Algonquin Anishinaabeg people.

www.ingramcontent.com/pod-product-compliance
Lightning Source LLC
Chambersburg PA
CBHW071211120626
46546CB00006B/2506